Why We Are in Need of Tales

Part II

Why We Are in Need of Tales

Part II

discovering philosophical treasures in picture books

Maria daVenza Tillmanns

IGUANA

Publisher: Meghan Behse
Editor: Holly Warren
Front cover image: Nayeli Garcia
Back cover image: Yesenia Perez

All drawings used with the permission of the artists and their parent(s).

ISBN 978-77180-514-8 (hardcover)
ISBN 978-77180-515-5 (paperback)
ISBN 978-77180-516-2 (ebook)

This is an original print edition of *Why We Are in Need of Tales, Part II*.

To all young dreamers

Why Dreams Are Important

There is a very important reason why we are in need of tales. Let me explain. See, a very, very long time ago, before we had tales, we had actual tails. These tails connected us to the world around us and to each other as well. We were able to communicate with each other with incredible nuance and accuracy — and just with the slightest touch or twitch of our tails. Imagine that!

Over the course of time, as we developed tools, we started to lose the need for our tails, and they became shorter and shorter until they disappeared altogether. And with their disappearance, we lost that mysterious connection to the world and to each other too. This was, of course, catastrophic, as we all now know.

In my little book called *Why We Are in Need of Tails*, Huk and Tuk — the main characters in the book — explain why we now need tales. They show us how tales can take the place of tails by helping us reconnect to the mystery of life.

Then, in my next little book, called *Why We Are in Need of Tales*, Huk and Tuk, who love sharing tales with each other, discuss six tales by Arnold Lobel and Leo Lionni.

This new little book shows us Huk and Tuk discussing six more of Lobel and Lionni's tales. In this book, they show the importance of why we are in need of dreams. See, dreams — in a mysterious way — also help us to reconnect to the world around us.

Dreams are kind of funny because they seem to come out of nowhere. But where is nowhere, you ask? I don't know, really, but I think our imaginations know somehow, because they can create things out of nowhere.

By the way, that's how Huk and Tuk came into existence. They materialized out of nowhere too.

See, dreams can spark our curiosity (by imagining what's on the other side) and ignite our fantasies (by imagining a world that can lift our spirits) and light up our creativity (by imagining the beauty expressed in art and music).

Or perhaps it's the other way around. Maybe curiosity, fantasy, and creativity spark dreams. What do you think? Either way, this is what these stories are about.

And did you know that one of the real geniuses of this world, Albert Einstein, believed that imagination is more important than knowledge? Think about it: Without imagination, we cannot create anything new. How dull would it be if everything were the same *all the time?*

Oh, and there's something else I need to tell you: In *Why We Are in Need of Tales*, Huk and Tuk also learn how important it is to keep your eyes wide open. Have you ever taken a walk through the woods? When you walk through the woods, you need to be able to see where you are going. You have to figure out what paths to take. Life is sort of like that too. In order to figure out what paths to take in life, or even what paths you *could* take in life, you need your eyes to be wide open.

Curiosity and imagination, as these next tales will show you, help you to keep your eyes wide open.

These tales are about the role dreams play in our lives. Dreams are like a third eye that helps us see things in so many *new* ways. That's really fascinating.

When we lost our tails, the mystery of life was sort of lost too. Thankfully, tales and dreams can help reconnect us with that mystery.

Why We Are in Need of Curiosity

— Tillie and the Wall by Leo Lionni —

Huk was over at Tuk's place enjoying the cool summer breeze while sitting on the little patio that Tuk had built.

Life can be so perfect at times for no particular reason.

Tuk lived on a hill, and from Tuk's house you could see the remnants of an old wall. Nobody knew why the wall was there, but everyone assumed it had served some purpose a long time ago.

Do you know what that wall was for? Huk asked.

No, Tuk replied. I've never really paid attention to it. I guess it's just always been there.

You know, Tuk continued, that reminds me of a tale about that exact thing: a wall that no one really paid attention to. There was this little mouse named Tillie who was the youngest in her family of mice.

What was special about Tillie was that she would see things nobody else ever did.

How did she do that? Huk asked.

She had her eyes wide open! Tuk exclaimed.

So, what did Tillie see that nobody else saw? Huk wanted to know. Really small things?

No, Tuk said, that's the surprising thing. Tillie noticed this humongous wall that everybody else just ignored. It was like they didn't even *see* that it was there.

I guess they figured it was part of the landscape, said Huk, and so they didn't give it a second thought. Just like you with that wall at the bottom of the hill.

Yes, exactly, said Tuk, but that's how Tillie was different. She always gave things a second thought. She was curious by nature.

And so, she was also really curious about the wall. She would always stare at the wall and wonder what was on the other side.

At night, when everybody else was asleep, Tillie would lie awake and imagine what could be on the other side of the wall — maybe there's a beautiful world over there with fantastical animals and plants. Who knows!

Tillie got so curious, Tuk continued, that she decided she *must* find out for herself what was on the other side of this huge wall.

She asked some of her friends to help her climb over the wall. She instructed them to stand on each other's shoulders, but even when they all stood as tall as they could and she climbed up to stand on her topmost friend's shoulders, Tillie still couldn't reach the top of the wall. The wall was *too tall*.

But Tillie was determined. This time, she decided to use a long rusty nail to poke a hole in the wall so she could peep through it and so her friends could peep through it too. They worked so hard trying to make a hole in the wall with the nail, but it didn't work. The wall was *too thick*.

Then she thought that they could go around the wall. Tillie and her friends walked and walked, looking for the end of the wall, but the wall was *too long*.

Her friends gave up, but Tillie didn't. Tillie got more and more curious and determined.

I guess I would too, Huk interjected.

Now this is where the story gets interesting, Tuk said, because one day Tillie noticed a worm digging a hole not far from the wall.

A light bulb went off in her little mouse head, and she thought, why hadn't anyone thought of this before?

Because Tillie's eyes were open with curiosity, she could see that the worm was showing her another way to the other side of the wall. And this time, Tillie thought, it may actually work.

She was so excited — wouldn't you be, Huk? — that she immediately started digging. Mice are really good at digging, so off she went.

She dug a long, deep tunnel under the wall. It was pitch black and very scary. She had no idea where she was going.

I think she's super brave, said Huk. Would you just go dig into the middle of nowhere? I know I wouldn't!

Maybe curiosity makes you brave, Tuk considered. This little mouse was on a mission and nothing was going to stop her.

Well, she finally made it to the other side, and you would not believe what she saw.

What did she see? asked Huk, who was totally wrapped up in the story and a bit scared too.

She saw mice, said Tuk. She saw a mouse family just like her own mouse family. Imagine that: after going on a long dig, you find creatures on the other side of the wall who are just like you.

The on-the-other-side-of-the-wall mice were also surprised and excited. They welcomed Tillie with a grand celebration.

And you know what else? Tuk said. Now these on-the-other-side-of-the-wall mice wanted to see what was on the other side of their wall too, and one by one, they followed Tillie back through the tunnel to her side of the wall.

That's a really interesting story, Huk decided. Tillie's imagination made her curious about what was on the other side of the wall — curious enough to try to find ways to get to the other side of it. And since she always gave things a second thought, she never gave up.

That's true, Tuk agreed. Her friends showed some interest, but they gave up after the first few things they tried didn't work. Only Tillie kept on trying to figure out what she could do to get to the other side.

Exactly! Huk said. And that's why she noticed the worm and discovered that tunneling was another method she could try.

And she took a real risk, Huk continued. Her own family of mice and the on-the-other-side-of-the-wall family of mice really admired her for what she did. And just look at the new world that opened up for all of them!

Tuk decided that both families now had a family on either side of the wall. Who would have guessed!

by Yesenia Perez

Why We Are in Need of Imagination

— *Cornelius* by Leo Lionni —

Huk and Tuk were getting a bit cold sitting outside on Tuk's patio, so they moved indoors and made a nice cup of hot tea.

Huk looked at Tuk and asked, do you remember Cornelius?

Hmm, Tuk responded, Cornelius who?

Cornelius, the young crocodile who walked upright, Huk said.

Upright, you say? Tuk asked. No, I don't think so.

Cornelius was a young croc who had just crawled out of his egg and onto the sandy beach along the river, Huk continued.

But unlike his siblings, who walked on all fours, Cornelius walked upright on his two hind legs.

That's peculiar, Tuk said.

That's right, said Huk, who went on to explain how as Cornelius grew taller and stronger — still walking on his two hind legs — he could see things no one else could. He was able to see way beyond the bushes.

And with his eyes wide open, Huk continued, he could see so far away. But his family was not interested in what he could see and just said things like, so what's so good about that? And when Cornelius could see the fish in the river from his higher vantage point, all his family said was, so what?

No one showed any interest in all the things Cornelius could see, or even any curiosity. He was so hurt and disappointed because his family didn't seem to care what he could do. And so, he wandered off.

Well, Tillie's family and friends never made fun of her, Tuk thought. Her friends even tried to help her get to the other side. They certainly weren't the sticks-in-the mud these crocs were. Blah!

So where did he go? Tuk wanted to know.

I'm not too sure, Huk said. I don't think the tale says, but it does say that soon after he wandered off, he saw a monkey sitting under a tree.

by Ricardo Alvarado

Cornelius, still excited about the world of wonders he could see while walking upright, said to the monkey, I can walk upright, you know, and see far away.

The monkey responded by saying, and I can stand on my head. And I can hang from my tail.

Cornelius was impressed. Cornelius could walk upright, but he could not do those things. So he asked the monkey to teach him.

The monkey was eager to help Cornelius learn his tricks. Because Cornelius could imagine himself doing those things, Huk said, he decided to practice and practice with the monkey's help. It took some work from both Cornelius and the monkey, though. Crocs are not meant to do these kinds of things. And maybe that's why the crocodile family showed no interest whatsoever. Crocs do what crocs do, and that's that.

Did Cornelius learn how to do what the monkey could do? Tuk asked.

Cornelius was determined, Huk said, and finally he learned how to stand on his head and hang from his tail, just as the monkey had taught him.

Cornelius was super proud now that he could do these tricks too, Huk continued. And so, he walked back to the beach along the river to show his family what he'd learned.

Uh-oh, said Tuk, that doesn't sound good.

Why? Huk asked.

Before he wandered off, Tuk said, his family couldn't care less that he could do things they could not, so why would they care now?

Maybe his family doesn't show any interest because they might see him as a show-off, Tuk continued, and maybe they even worry that he thinks he is better than they are.

Do you think he's a show-off? Tuk asked.

Huk took a sip of tea and responded, I don't know what his family thinks, but *I* don't think Cornelius is a show-off. Cornelius was simply excited about what he could do, and he really wanted to learn these tricks from the monkey.

He could imagine himself learning new things all the time. I mean, when the monkey said to him that he could stand on his head and hang from his tail,

Cornelius *could* have responded like his family did by saying something like, so what? Or, what's so good about that? Or, I'm a croc and you're a monkey and we cannot do the same things.

But because he could imagine himself being able to do these monkey tricks too, he asked the monkey to teach him and help him accomplish these things crocodiles simply don't do. Have *you* ever seen a crocodile hang from its tail?

I get it, said Tuk, because when Cornelius told his family he could see things far away when he walked upright, they too could have asked him how to walk upright, so they could see far away too.

I think Cornelius just wanted to share what he knew, Huk said, and that's also why he was eager to go back to the beach along the river where his family lived.

So, what happened then? How did his family react? Tuk wanted to know.

Well, they reacted exactly the way you would expect such a stick-in-the mud family to react: When Cornelius showed them that he could stand on his head and hang from his tail, all they could say was — once again — so what?

As you would expect, Huk said, Cornelius was — once again — hurt and disappointed. He decided to leave these uninspired crocs to themselves and to go back to be with the monkey. At least he and the monkey were friends, and they could share their cool tricks.

But as he started to walk away — still upright — he glanced over his shoulder and saw something amazing: his brothers and sisters were falling over each other trying to stand on their heads and hang from their tails.

Really! Tuk exclaimed. They were jealous of Cornelius? Did they really just want to be able to do all the things Cornelius could do too?

Huk nodded and said, it seems so.

Then why didn't they ask Cornelius to teach them just like Cornelius had asked the monkey to teach him?

That's an interesting question, Huk said. What do you think?

Maybe his sisters and brothers did kind of admire Cornelius but did not want to look like fools trying to do the things Cornelius did, Tuk replied. Sometimes we don't want to try new things because we don't want to feel embarrassed when we can't do them.

But somehow Cornelius doesn't really care if he looks like a fool. He just keeps on trying and keeps on practicing until he can do these tricks too.

Huk smiled. That sounds a little like when Tillie found a way to get to the other side of the wall.

How so? Tuk asked.

Well, Tuk, just like Tillie, Cornelius never gave up, Huk said.

And they didn't give up because they were curious and could imagine things beyond what they knew already. And a whole new world opened up because of it.

by Yesenia Perez

Why We Are in Need of Nighttime Dreams

— *The Dream* by Arnold Lobel —

The next day, Huk and Tuk went to see a play called "The Dream."

Huk and Tuk know that everyone has dreams big and small, and dreams influence how we think and feel and sometimes even how we live our lives. So they decided that seeing a play about dreams would be very inspiring.

When Huk and Tuk got to the theater, Frog and Toad were there. Toad was going to be on stage that night. Frog was in the audience and was eagerly awaiting his best friend's performance.

Soon Toad appeared on stage. He looked like he belonged in a Shakespearean play with his incredibly colorful outfit, boots and wide-rimmed hat with a plume hanging from his chapeau. He was a toad of consequence, and everyone in the audience was in awe.

Huk looked at Tuk and nodded in admiration. This is going to be some play, Huk whispered.

Then they heard a loud voice announce: Presenting the greatest toad in the world.

Frog, seated in a front-row seat, started clapping. He agreed that Toad was indeed the greatest toad ever.

Toad took a deep bow and sat at the piano.

The voice then announced: Toad will now play the piano very well.

Frog, who could not help himself, cried out, hooray for Toad!

Toad started playing the piano and was magnificent. He didn't miss a note.

Frog, cried Toad, can you play the piano like this? No, said Frog.

When Toad looked into the audience, he spotted his friend Frog.

Huk and Tuk noticed that Toad looked puzzled after he saw Frog, so they looked over. Tuk leaned over to Huk and whispered, does Frog look smaller to you?

by Adrian Cacho

I'm not sure, Huk replied, looking a bit concerned. Then Huk whispered, I thought this play was going to be about dreams.

Maybe we should wait and see, Tuk whispered.

Again, the same voice came on and announced: Toad will now walk on a high wire and he will not fall down.

Huk and Tuk saw Toad perform this dangerous feat with ease.

Toad called out to Frog and asked if this was something he could do. Again, Frog said no, he couldn't.

Huk and Tuk noticed that after Toad was done walking on the high wire, he looked into the audience at Frog. Toad looked worried. Huk and Tuk followed Toad's gaze to where Frog was sitting. Frog seemed smaller still. Then they too looked really worried. Huk and Tuk didn't know what was going on.

Was this all a dream?

Huk and Tuk had gone to see a play called "The Dream," or so they thought. Were they now the ones dreaming?

by Ethan Hernandez

How about the rest of the audience? Were they watching a play, or were they *in* a play?

The announcer came on again and said: Toad will now dance, and it will be wonderful.

When Huk and Tuk looked over to where Frog sat, there was no one there. Frog had disappeared.

Huk gasped. What just happened, Tuk? Frog is gone!

This was certainly the strangest play they had ever seen, and they got scared.

But it wasn't just Huk and Tuk who got scared.

Frog! Toad cried. Frog, where are you? Toad sounded desperate.

Let's go home, Huk suggested. I don't like this play. This play is a nightmare, not a dream.

Meanwhile, Toad panicked, and while the announcer started to say something like, and now the greatest toad will..., Toad ran off the stage looking for Frog.

At that point, Huk and Tuk got up and left the theater. They were not interested in the ending.

When they got outside, Huk looked at Tuk and said, oh boy, that was weird, and Huk gave Tuk a big hug to make sure Tuk was real and hadn't disappeared.

I can't wait to get home and have some hot chocolate to calm my nerves, Huk said.

When they were settled in at Huk's place, drinking their hot chocolate, Huk asked, but why did Frog get smaller and smaller?

I think, Tuk replied, that maybe when someone boasts about how they are the best, it makes their friends feel small.

And when Toad realized that he might have lost his friend in the process of bragging about how great he was, he panicked. He didn't want to lose his best friend Frog.

So "The Dream" was really about how important friendships are — maybe even how they are the most important? asked Huk.

As they drank their hot chocolate in silence, Huk and Tuk both looked discombobulated. They were imagining how Toad felt not seeing Frog in the audience anymore. What if they each looked over at the other and there was no one there?

Tuk thought, what if Huk disappeared?

Huk thought, what if Tuk disappeared?

They had to stop imagining what this might feel like. This was horrible!

It wasn't until they had finished their hot chocolate that they looked at each other, so happy they were sitting there together as best friends who wouldn't *dream* of being without each other.

Huk and Tuk are still not quite sure whether they had been watching a play called "The Dream" or actually dreaming they were watching a play called "The Dream." Whatever it was, it had made them aware and woke them up — with eyes wide open — to how very important real friendship is.

Why We Are in Need of Daytime Dreams

— *Frederick* by Leo Lionni —

One morning, Tuk went over to Huk's place for breakfast. They had some nice warm toast with jam and hot coffee.

It was frigid out. The cold made Tuk think of a tale about a mouse named Frederick. Huk, Tuk said, do you know the tale about Frederick the daydreamer mouse? Frederick who didn't prepare for winter in the same way the other mice did?

No, said Huk, I don't know about any daydreamer mouse. Tell me about him.

Frederick, Tuk began, lived with his mouse family in the crumbling wall below my house. I've seen them scurrying about many times. The story starts in the fall when all the mice were gathering supplies like nuts and wheat and straw and preparing for the winter months. All the mice except Frederick, that is. Frederick didn't join them.

Didn't he help out? Huk asked. Did he just loaf around instead?

That's exactly what he was accused of doing, Tuk replied. He sat in the sun instead.

Why? Huk interjected.

Frederick told the others that he was gathering sunrays for the cold dark days of winter. He reassured them that he too was hard at work. But they didn't seem to believe him.

Would you believe Frederick, Huk? Or would you accuse him of being lazy and of making up silly excuses to not help out?

Not knowing quite what to say, Huk did not reply. It seemed to Huk that Frederick should have helped out, but then again, why not believe him when he said he was hard at work too?

While he sat on a stone, staring at the meadow, Tuk continued, Frederick told the other mice that he was gathering colors for when the days became gray and dreary.

So, was he working hard like the other mice or not? Huk asked.

Well, that depends on what you mean by work, I guess, Tuk replied.

That didn't sound all that convincing to Huk. Work meant *doing* things, like gathering nuts and storing them in the crevices of the wall. Sitting on a stone and gathering sunrays or colors didn't sound like work at all.

So, what else did Frederick do — or rather, not do? Huk wanted to know.

Tuk told Huk that Frederick once seemed half asleep, and the other mice thought he was dreaming. Are you dreaming? the mice asked. Oh no! Frederick said. I am gathering words for when nobody has anything left to say during the long, cold winter.

Finally, the winter set in and the mice disappeared into their cozy little hideout in the wall.

For a while, the straw kept them warm, and they had lots to eat. They told each other stories about foxes and such, and they were happy.

But as the winter carried on, they had less and less to eat. It seemed colder than before, and no one felt like telling stories anymore.

But then they remembered Frederick and asked him about *his* supplies.

Huk was curious how this was going to play out and urged Tuk to continue.

Frederick told the other mice to close their eyes and imagine the warm glow of the sunrays, said Tuk.

As Frederick spoke of the sun, the other mice did start feeling a little better when they imagined how the sun warmed their bodies. They weren't sure if it was Frederick's words as he spoke or some kind of magic that caused it.

Then Frederick told them to imagine the colors of the blue periwinkles, the red poppies, the yellow wheat and the green leaves. Suddenly, the winter didn't seem so gray anymore.

Huk was impressed. The power of imagination was nothing to sneeze at. It really could make you feel better.

The mice were impressed too and asked Frederick about the words he had gathered up. Then he recited a poem he had created in his head from the words he had gathered.

The mice were convinced that Frederick's hard work *had* paid off and *had* helped them all get through the rough, cold winter after all.

Huk liked this story and decided that without imagination, life would be quite unbearable, even if you had enough to eat.

So, is imagination something like food for thought? Huk wondered. Huk thought that expression said it all — imagination was a kind of food for the mind and, just like food, it helped them get through the bitter, cold winter.

As though Tuk could read Huk's thoughts, Tuk said, imagination creates thoughts and feelings from what we can't always see; it exists in our mind. I mean, we need a mind's eye to see it. And with their mind's eye, the family of mice was able to somehow feel the glow of the warm sun, see the beautiful and vibrant colors of the flowers and feel the soothing effects of Frederick's poetry.

In that way, Frederick helped his family get through the winter, not by collecting food or straw, but by transporting them through their imaginations to a world way beyond the bitter cold.

by Nayeli Garcia

Why We Are in Need of Creativity

— Matthew's Dream **by Leo Lionni —**

After Huk and Tuk's strange experience at the theater, they decided to visit the Metropolitan Mouse Museum — the MeMo Museum for short.

They had heard about the great artwork of a new artist by the name of Matthew and were eager to go see his famous paintings.

Huk and Tuk made a delicious lunch to take along, and then they headed to the MeMo Museum.

On the way, Huk told Tuk a little bit about this new artist.

Matthew, Huk began, was an only child in his mouse family. And in a corner of the attic where they lived, he had gathered a bunch of stuff — books, magazines, pieces of an old lamp and a broken doll. They called it "Matthew's corner."

Matthew's family was very, very poor and could not afford nice things.

His parents would ask Matthew repeatedly, what do you want to be when you grow up? They were secretly hoping Matthew would say his life's dream was to become a doctor or lawyer and they would become very, very rich and be able to afford Parmesan cheese and other delicacies.

Matthew was curious about the world beyond the attic where his family lived, and he said, I don't know what I want to be. I want to see the world.

That didn't sound overly encouraging to Matthew's family, but Matthew was still young and in school, so they didn't push the issue.

One day, Huk continued, Matthew and his classmates went to the MeMo Museum.

The mouse artwork was spectacular. The portraits of famous mice, the still lifes of fruit and Parmesan cheese, and the landscapes of mountains and rivers enthralled Matthew. Then his class came to a gallery of abstract art. Matthew had never seen art like that before, and he found it intriguing and exciting.

by Edgar Parada

As he looked at the abstract art, Matthew realized that the world he'd always wanted to see was right there in front of him. This world was alive with vibrant colors, and with all kinds of shapes dancing across the canvas.

While Matthew was strolling through the abstract art gallery, he met a mouse named Nicoletta, who also thought the art was wonderful and inspiring.

When Matthew got home from his field trip to the MeMo Museum, he felt so happy. The museum had felt like home. The paintings he'd seen had excited him and made sense to him.

That night, he dreamed that the world had become one huge painting, and he and Nicoletta walked through it hand in hand.

Let's stay here forever, he whispered to her in his dream.

When he woke up, he found himself back in his little corner of the attic. All the beauty in his dream had vanished. He felt alone and lonely, and he cried.

But then his little eyes suddenly opened wide, and everything started to change around him. Instead

by Adrian Cacho

of junk, he saw colors and shapes similar to what he had seen in the museum. The doll's hair was golden and her dress a beautiful green. The magazine covers were splashed with vibrant colors, and spreading out from the cobwebs were subtle silver threads. It was as though magic had turned his little corner into a whole new world. It had come *alive* too.

Then he ran to his parents, so the story goes, and told them he wanted to become a painter. And that's what he did! He worked hard and became the best painter he could be.

Wow! said Tuk. He made his dream come true.

That's right, Huk said. Matthew lived out his dream: he ended up seeing the world by becoming a famous painter. He also married Nicoletta. And, to his family's delight, he could afford Parmesan cheese, which they happily feasted on every night.

His most famous painting is in the museum we're going to today, said Huk. It's called "My Dream."

Hmm, said Tuk, so not only did Matthew become a creative artist, his creativity helped him to see the world beyond his little corner up in the attic.

by Marcos Maldonado

Creativity opened up his eyes wide and his little world became so big.

But what *is* creativity, Huk? Tuk wanted to know.

Well, said Huk, creativity, I think, is like imagination and curiosity and dreaming because it creates something that wasn't there before.

I'm not sure I understand, said Tuk. How does it work?

If you think about it, Huk continued, Tillie was curious about what was behind that huge wall and discovered a whole new world existed beyond it. Cornelius imagined himself doing tricks nobody in his family had ever thought of doing. You see what I'm saying?

I think so, said Tuk. Frederick gathered up a world of colors and warm sunrays and words that helped his family get beyond the world of the bitter, cold winter. And Matthew created a whole new world beyond his little corner in the attic.

I see, Tuk concluded. They did all create something out of nothing.

Why We Are in Need of Art

— Geraldine, The Music Mouse by Leo Lionni —

It was a long day at the MeMo Museum. When Huk and Tuk finally got home, they cooked a wonderful meal. It had so many different colored vegetables in it that it too looked like a colorful abstract painting.

Art is so inspiring, Huk said. It makes everything come alive, don't you think?

It actually does, Tuk said. Let me tell you about another great artist by the name of Geraldine. She makes music come alive.

Geraldine is a musician. Have you heard of her?

I have, said Huk. I have heard her music. She plays the flute, and her music is like a dream.

Geraldine was a mouse who had never heard music before, so how she became a musician is an interesting story, Tuk said.

Huk was confused. Could she not hear the sound of music, or was there simply never any music in her life?

The tale doesn't say, Tuk answered. She could hear noises and the peeping of other mice, but music? Never!

Anyway, Tuk continued, Geraldine lived in a big house, and this house had a pantry.

Amazing, Huk interjected, because mice love pantries.

That's so true, returned Tuk. So one day when Geraldine went looking in the pantry, she saw a huge piece of Parmesan cheese. Her eyes grew big, and she desperately wanted to take the cheese to her hideout, but she didn't know how to do it.

She decided to tell her friends about the cheese. That's what friends are for.

Friends are for helping you steal cheese? Huk asked dubiously.

Or, Tuk said, friends are for helping you out.

Helping you out to do what? Huk persisted.

Anyway, Tuk continued, Geraldine's friends were eager to help, and off they all marched to the pantry. Parmesan could not be passed up.

by Edgar Parada

With a lot of community effort, they were able to push, pull and drag the huge piece of cheese to Geraldine's hideout.

Immediately, she went to the top of the block of cheese and started nibbling piece by piece, chunk after chunk.

Her friends, excited to see that much Parmesan cheese, started carrying off bits of the cheese. What a treat this was!

But when Geraldine looked at the cheese, she noticed that the shapes of two giant mouse ears had appeared where she had been nibbling away. She seemed to have sculpted the cheese into what looked like a mouse without even realizing it.

And as she kept on nibbling away, she saw that the mouse was holding its tail to its lips, the way someone would hold a flute. Remember, though, Geraldine had never seen or heard a flute.

So how did she do it? Huk asked.

It's a mystery, Tuk replied. She had created an incredible sculpture without even realizing, and somehow the mouse in the sculpture was playing an instrument she didn't know anything about.

by Ricardo Alvarado

Not surprisingly, Geraldine was exhausted from all the work and soon fell asleep.

And not long after that, she was awakened by some wonderful sounds — sounds that seemed to come from the mouse's tail flute. Was she dreaming?

Well, was she dreaming? Huk asked.

The story is that she was wide awake when she heard those beautiful sounds, Tuk replied. Or she at least felt wide awake in her dream. And she could clearly hear the music coming from the mouse sculpture.

She was in awe.

But then another strange thing happened, Tuk continued. As the night slowly turned to day, the music started to fade as well. But every night, when it started to get dark, the music started once again. This went on for several days.

And then Geraldine started to hear the music during the day too. It was lingering in her head, and she started to recognize the melodies.

Her friends, who had run out of food, came running back to Geraldine hoping she would share more cheese with them.

Geraldine did not know what to do. Her music mouse was made of cheese and her friends were hungry and wanted to eat the sculpture.

What a hard decision to make! Huk exclaimed. So, what happened?

Geraldine did not know how to explain why she didn't want her friends eating the sculpture, Tuk continued, so she simply blurted out, because it's music!

What's music? her friends asked. Geraldine was again unable to explain.

But then she thought of something. Geraldine took her tail and held it to her lips. She started to blow on her tail. Nothing but noise — not music — came from her efforts, and her friends started to make fun of her. So, this is music? they jeered.

Geraldine was terribly hurt but decided not to give up.

Slowly, a beautiful sound came from her lips. It *was* music!

Her friends were amazed and decided that they could not ask Geraldine to give them chunks of the music mouse to eat.

But then, to everybody's surprise, Geraldine said, since the music is now in me, you can take as much cheese as you want.

Geraldine kept on playing her tail flute while her friends nibbled away at the Parmesan cheese.

That's how she became a musician, Tuk said. Isn't that interesting?

Very, said Huk, and in this tale too, something came out of nothing. Music came out of the mouse's tail — her actual tail. The tail became a flute. That doesn't just happen.

A tale came out of a tail, Tuk mused.

In all these dream tales, something new was created — something larger and more beautiful and more exciting.

But it didn't just happen, Huk decided. It took courage. Tillie needed courage to dig a tunnel under the wall in the dark, not knowing where she'd end up. And Cornelius needed courage to not be afraid of looking like a fool trying to do impossible tricks — impossible for a young croc, that is.

by Marcos Maldonado

And, Tuk added, we found out that it takes courage to be vulnerable within a friendship and fight for it. That play or dream — or *whatever* it was — showed us that you can lose a deep friendship if you take it for granted.

That's right. And what about Frederick? To continue to do what he was doing while others thought he was doing nothing at all and kind of scorned him for not helping to gather food for the winter, Huk continued, that couldn't have been easy. And it took courage for Matthew to dream big and dare to become a painter.

I think, Tuk said, that they all needed courage to be creative. Geraldine also looked foolish when she tried to make music with her tail. They all needed the courage to go against others — their family and friends even — who didn't understand or appreciate what they were doing, and the courage to persist when they failed. They needed courage to go it alone. Because they alone could see something most others could not.

So why are we in need of dreams? Huk asked. Do dreams give us courage?

Yes, Tuk replied. Dreams give us the courage to take risks and to persist and to not be afraid but rather inspired to go beyond what is familiar and venture into worlds created by our imagination. Dreams help us come *alive*!

That makes sense, Tuk said. And tales — or tails, as we knew them — connect us to these wonderful worlds we can see with our imagination, our mind's eye, and connect us to the mystery we call life.

References

Lionni, Leo. *Cornelius*. New York: Dragonfly Books, 1983.

——. *Frederick*. New York: Dragonfly Books, 1967.

——. *Geraldine, the Music Mouse*. New York: Dragonfly Books, 1979.

——. *Matthew's Dream*. New York: Dragonfly Books, 1991.

——. *Tillie and the Wall*. New York: Dragonfly Books, 1989.

Lobel, Arnold. "The Dream" in *Frog and Toad Together*. New York: Harper & Row Publishers, 1972.

Acknowledgements

First and foremost, I would like to acknowledge the students and teachers at El Toyon Elementary School in National City, California. For three years, I conducted classes in philosophy with students from first, second and third grade. First, I would read a picture book story with the students, then they would work in small groups to philosophize about some of the questions that came up for them in the story. Finally, they would write and draw their thoughts about the story and the questions it raised. During those three years, I worked with Yen Dang, Silvia Toledo, Patricia Carrillo, Pat Duran and Elizabeth McEvoy. These teachers truly saw the value of doing philosophy with children, encouraging the children to ask questions they are curious about and think for themselves. Naturally, these skills spill over into anything the students are required to learn in school and beyond. This year, during the pandemic, I continued working with Patricia Carrillo who would do a read-aloud of one of the stories discussed by Huk and Tuk and ask the children to draw their thoughts and feelings about the story. Last year, we received permission to use the children's drawings as illustrations for *Why We Are in Need of Tales, Part I*, and this year, we will use drawings from Ms. Carrillo's class for *Why We Are in Need of Tales, Part II*. Once again, I am always grateful for the feedback from my friend and colleague Claartje van Sijl and, of course, from Mr. Lizzard. I want to thank Iguana Books, especially its publisher, Meghan Behse, and my editor, Holly Warren, who has been a delight to work with. If anyone gets what Huk and Tuk are about, it's Holly.

Maria daVenza Tillmanns

Maria teaches a "Philosophy with Children" program in underserved San Diego schools in partnership with the University of California, San Diego. In 1980, she attended Dr. Matthew Lipman's workshop on philosophy for children and later wrote her dissertation on philosophical counseling and teaching under the direction of Martin Buber scholar Dr. Maurice Friedman. She has publications in a number of international journals. For Maria, philosophy is an art form, and she enjoys painting with ideas. Philosophy has helped her navigate the world in all its complexity, including having a multicultural background and having been raised in the US as well as in the Netherlands. She came back to the US to study and moved across the Atlantic multiple times.